Prehistoric Britain

Skara Brae

Dawn Finch

raintree
a Capstone company — publishers for children

Raintree is an imprint of Capstone Global Library Limited, a company incorporated in England and Wales having its registered office at 7 Pilgrim Street, London, EC4V 6LB – Registered company number: 6695582

www.raintree.co.uk
myorders@raintree.co.uk

Edited by Helen Cox Cannons
Designed by Steve Mead
Original illustrations © Capstone Global Library Limited 2015
Picture research by Wanda Winch
Production by Victoria Fitzgerald
Originated by Capstone Global Library Limited
Printed and bound in China by CTPS

ISBN 978 1 474 70924 8
19 18 17 16 15
10 9 8 7 6 5 4 3 2 1

British Library Cataloguing in Publication Data
A full catalogue record for this book is available from the British Library.

Acknowledgements
We would like to thank the following for permission to reproduce photographs: all images courtesy of Dawn Finch except SCRAN Trust: Orkney Islands Council, p26.

The author would like to thank Andrew Burnet (Contents Editor and Standards Manager for Historic Scotland), Kirsty Owen (Archaeologist, Historic Scotland), Mary Dunnett (Site Manager, Skara Brae) and Fiona Grahame (Site Guide, Skara Brae) for their invaluable help in the preparation of this book.

Contents

Some words in this book appear in bold, **like this**. You can find out what they mean by looking in the glossary.

Where is Skara Brae?

Skara Brae is one of the **prehistoric** sites to be found on a group of Scottish islands called the Orkney Islands. The Orkney Islands lie about 16 kilometres (10 miles) off the north coast of Scotland.

The site of the village of Skara Brae was lived on for c.600 years, some time between around 3200 BC to 2500 BC. At this time, people had just started to settle in permanent, or long-lasting, homes. This was during the period of time known as the **Neolithic** period. Neolithic means "New Stone Age", which means that it was the end of the Stone Age.

Historians believe that there could have been as many as 10,000 people living in the Orkney Islands during the Neolithic period.

Building a picture

Neolithic people did not have a written language that we understand. What we know about them comes from the objects that they have left behind.

Archaeologists and historians have studied the remains of Skara Brae's buildings and the people's belongings and even bones. Thanks to their studies, we now know a lot about life on Skara Brae.

The Orkney Islands and Skara Brae can be seen on this map.

The weather can be very bad in Orkney. Thousands of years of storms had covered the **abandoned** village with sand. Nobody knew about it.

In the winter of 1850, a huge storm came in from the sea and uncovered an ancient **mound**. After the storm had passed, people could see the ruins of the ancient village. Over the next 150 years, the site was **excavated** a number of times (see page 26). Ten buildings were properly uncovered. The site now has nine houses and a large building.

How do we know about Skara Brae?

The area where Skara Brae was built would have been a lively place in the **Neolithic** period. It was a fishing and farming community. Possibly around 100 people lived there.

Where there are many people, there is a lot of rubbish! These Neolithic people let their rubbish rot down to **midden**. Midden was like a rubbish heap that mainly contained bone, shell, stone and waste. People used the midden as a building material. Their houses had two stone walls: an inner one and an outer one, with a gap in between. The gap was then packed with the midden material. This made the wall thick and weatherproof.

Archaeologists think that the Neolithic midden material kept out the cold and made the houses much stronger.

Midden was also packed into the spaces between the houses, making part of them sit underground. This sheltered the houses from the cold winds. The midden has been very useful to **archaeologists,** as they have found many interesting objects in it. People throw away all sorts of things and these help us to understand what life was really like in Skara Brae.

Building with rubbish

It sounds strange to us, but many ancient people used their rubbish to build with! There were not many trees on Orkney, so people used whatever they could to support the walls of their houses. Midden probably would not have been very smelly, as it was rotted down like compost, and then mixed with earth and sand.

The people of Skara Brae

The **Neolithic** period lasted from around 4000 BC to 2000 BC. The people of this time had not yet discovered metal to make their tools. Instead, their tools were made of stone, animal bones and horns.

The people who lived at Skara Brae probably first came from the mainland of Northern Scotland or Northern Europe. In around 3000 BC, more houses were built and the people began to plant crops, breed animals and hunt and fish. These were the first farming **settlements** on Orkney.

Neolithic people made tools like these from stone, animal bones and horn.

Driftwood like this washed up on the shore. It was used to make handles for tools.

Orkney can have warmer weather than mainland Scotland. This is thanks to a warm current of air and water called the Gulf Stream. The land on Skara Brae was also very good for farming.

Neolithic farmers on the Scottish mainland often had to chop down trees in an area to make it ready for farming.

Wood

Wood for building and fires was rare in Orkney. The Neolithic **Orcadians** used **driftwood** that they found on the beaches. Experts believe that some wood they were using had come all the way from North America – carried there by the strong Atlantic currents!

The houses

All of the nine houses of Skara Brae are round in shape and had one room. They have **alcoves** built into the walls and a pit for fires in the middle of the room. The houses were quite large and were separate at first. Over time, they became joined together by covered passageways. The doors were very low – people would have had to crouch down or even crawl to get through the doorways.

Each house had a large piece of stone furniture called a dresser. It faced the door and would have been the first thing that a person saw when entering the house. Nobody knows exactly what dressers were for. They may have been used to display items that people were proud of. Houses also had other stone furniture. These included bed frames, storage boxes and a firepit, known as a **hearth** (see page 12).

Dresser

All of the stone dressers are roughly the same size and built in the same way.

This is a bed frame. Each house has two beds, one on each side of the room.

Beds

A stone bed does not look very comfortable, but all that is left today is the frame of the bed. People who lived at Skara Brae would have used dried plants, such as bracken or heather, to fill the stone bed frames. Then they would have put sheepskin or fur on top. Many of the beds have small cupboards built into the wall above them. The people might have used them to store their personal items.

Cells

Archaeologists call the alcoves along the walls "cells". Some of these cells are in places that are easy to reach, but some are tucked away behind the dressers. Archaeologists are not sure what the cells were used for, but they think some must have been used for storage. In one of the cells, archaeologists found over 3,250 beads. Some cells have drains running underneath them. This means that those cells might have been used as toilets.

Hearth

The **hearths** would have been used for both cooking and warming the house. They would have been very smoky. With no windows, the houses would have been quite dark, with very little fresh air inside. Roofs were probably high enough to hang fish or meat over the fire to **cure** in the smoke.

With no windows in the house, the fire in the hearth would also help to light up the room.

The houses are linked by narrow covered passageways. This means that the people must have been able to move from house to house without going outside.

The doors were made from large slabs of stone or wooden slats that were pushed into place to block the gap. The people put bars across the doors to lock them in place. These fitted into slots on the walls and were made of whalebone or wood. The doors could only be locked from the inside.

The passageways are very narrow and would have been covered.

Fuel

Evidence from other **Neolithic** and Stone Age sites shows that people burned animal dung (poo) as fuel. They also used all sorts of other things for fuel, such as dried heather and bracken, whalebone and dried seaweed.

Food and farming

The people of Skara Brae were farmers. The remains from the **midden** show that they kept animals. The bones that have been found are quite hard to identify, but **archaeologists** think that they kept cattle, sheep and goats.

Seabirds

The midden contained a lot of eggshell that can only have come from the seabirds that nest on the cliffs. Archaeologists have found **evidence** that the people ate many different wild seabirds, including gannets, auks, guillemots and eider ducks.

These birds nest on steep cliffs. It would have been dangerous gathering these eggs. People would need to be lowered over the edge to collect them!

Archaeologists think that these stone boxes were used to hold water. They would soak **limpets** in them, which would keep them soft and fresh. They used limpets as fishing bait.

People hunted wild deer, both for food and to use the skins and antlers. The farmers grew barley. Some historians think that they might have used this to bake a sort of bread. On a nearby island, called Rousay, archaeologists found small ovens built into the houses.

Seafood

The people of Skara Brae enjoyed eating freshwater and sea fish. We know this because a lot of fish bones have been found in the midden. They ate plenty of cod and a type of fish called coley, but they also sometimes ate crab, mussels, sea urchins, oysters and lobster. The people of Skara Brae would have been well fed. They had plenty of fresh water from the freshwater **loch** and even had milk from their cows and sheep.

Clothing and jewellery

It is very difficult to know exactly what the people of Skara Brae wore because nothing remains of their clothing. **Archaeologists** have found many small tools at the site, including pins and awls made from bone. An awl was a small, sharply pointed tool used to make holes in leather or wood. Finding these tools shows us that people were sewing and pinning together pieces of fur and animal skin to make their clothes. There is some **evidence** to show that the people of Skara Brae may have captured otters to use their fur.

The pins that have been found were probably used to fasten clothing. Many of the pins are made from walrus tusk. This means that it is likely that walrus were breeding on the island during this time.

Hundreds of bone pins were found at Skara Brae.

Paint pots

Small pots made from shell, bone and stone were found at the site. Some of the pots still contained the remains of a rust-coloured **pigment** called red **ochre**. Ochre had been mixed with animal fat and rolled into a ball. People may have used it to decorate their bodies.

Beads

It seems that the people of Skara Brae cared a great deal about their appearance. As well as finding pins at the site, archaeologists have also found pendants. A pendant is a piece of jewellery that hangs on a necklace.

Thousands of beads have been found. It is possible that these were once sewn onto clothing for decoration. As well as loose beads, archaeologists have found beads that would have been strung together to make necklaces. Many of the beads are made from the bones and teeth of sea mammals.

Life in the village

Life at Skara Brae would have been busy. Running the farms and fishing would have taken up most of the people's time. If they had simple lamps they would have been fuelled with animal fat, so would not be very bright. In Orkney, the days are very long at midsummer but very short at midwinter, so the people would have spent a lot of wintertime in darkness.

Archaeologists are not sure what these carvings mean. They might have just been for decoration.

The houses seem to have been well taken care of. The people made deep scratches or carvings on some of the walls and furniture. This may have been for decoration. It is possible that the paint found at Skara Brae was also used to decorate the walls.

Medicine

The people of Skara Brae were able to treat their own injuries. They will have been able to use plants as medicine. **Archaeologists** found a large amount of dried puffballs at the site. Puffballs are found in rough ground and are related to mushrooms. The inside of a puffball mushroom looks a bit like cotton wool. It can be used to stop bleeding and treat cuts.

Games and music

We cannot be sure if the people of Skara Brae played games, but a number of carved animal knucklebones have been found. These may have been used for playing games, but they could also have been used for religious uses. A piece of carved bone was found at the site. Archaeologists think that this may have been some kind of flute or musical instrument.

Puffballs, like these, were used to treat bleeding.

Community

No weapons have been found at the Skara Brae site. There is also no sign of any kind of **defensive** wall or ditch around the village. This could possibly show that the people did not live in fear of an attack. However, we will never know this for sure.

The people of Skara Brae probably had a strong sense of community, as they lived together very closely. They would have hunted, farmed and spent time with people in their own village and also those from nearby villages.

The Marketplace

The people of Skara Brae paved an area with flat stones. The area has been called the Marketplace. However, there is no **evidence** to show that it was actually a market. It is likely that this would have been a gathering place for people to meet.

Even though the Marketplace was in the open air, it was surrounded by high walls and sheltered from the wind.

One of the buildings at Skara Brae has been called the Workshop. It does not have a dresser or beds like the other buildings, but it does have a large **hearth**. The floor of this building was covered with small bits of chert. Chert is a stone found on Orkney that is like flint. The people of Skara Brae used chert to make tools. The amount of chert found in Workshop shows us that this was probably a tool workshop.

Workshop

The Workshop is a larger building than the houses and was built at a later date. It may have been built so that the people had somewhere to work together outside their homes. It was not built into the **midden** like the houses and has thicker walls.

Religion and beliefs

In Orkney, there are many other **Neolithic** sites, including large burial **mounds.** These burial mounds are built with stone and covered in earth and grass. We are not sure exactly what Neolithic people believed in. However, we do know that they took great care when they were burying their dead. This tells us that caring for the dead was important to them.

Archaeologists have not yet found where the people of Skara Brae buried their dead. The burial place may have been washed away by the sea.

Strange objects

Lots of carved stone objects have been found at Skara Brae and other sites around Orkney. Archaeologists do not know what these objects were used for. They may have been for religious uses or may have just been used for games.

Maeshowe

The biggest mound on the Orkney Islands is called Maeshowe. From the outside, it looks like a large, grassy hill. Inside it, there is a stone tomb. The opening of the tomb catches the light at sunset in midwinter. This shows us that the movement of the Sun and Moon was important to the people.

Brodgar

The houses of Skara Brae were all the same shape and style. This suggests there was no village or religious leader living there. A large group of buildings have recently been found near the village. They seem to be part of what was a temple-like place. At the Ness of Brodgar, archaeologists have uncovered the remains of a walled area. They believe this was used as a religious site.

The Ring of Brodgar is a stone circle. Large slabs of stone were stood upright on purpose and placed in a large circle. These circles were probably very important in ancient times.

A village abandoned

At some time around 2500 BC, the villagers **abandoned** Skara Brae. At first, **archaeologists** thought that the people had run away from a great storm. However, that idea has been proved unlikely. If the villagers had done that, they would have returned after the storm and dug out the rest of their belongings.

Many belongings were found in the village, but not as many as there might have been if it had still been lived in. Archaeologists are sure that the layer of sand found in the village had built up gradually and not covered the village all in one go. This means that it is more likely that the people moved away over time, as the population grew older.

During the Neolithic period, Skara Brae would have been about 1 kilometre (0.6 mile) from the sea. Today, the sea is so close that sometimes stormy waves hit the houses.

Seawater can flood the land and turn it into salt marsh. The people would not have been able to carry on farming on this land.

Changing land

Skara Brae was further inland during the **Neolithic** period. Over thousands of years, fierce storms have washed the land away. There are many possible reasons why the people left Skara Brae. They could have left the village because the land around them was no longer as **fertile**. This could happen because the salty spray from the sea would make the land too salty to grow crops.

It is also possible that the people just wanted to live further inland. The people may have lost their freshwater **loch** to the sea. Living in the village would have been harder without easy access to fresh water. Also, the younger people of Skara Brae may have left to find new farmland of their own. Archaeologists think that they may have moved to newer **settlements**.

Excavation

After the storm of 1850, the ruins of Skara Brae were discovered by William Watt of Skaill. William Watt was the local landowner there. He began to explore the site. By 1868, his staff had managed to clear the sand from four of the houses.

In December 1924, another huge storm revealed even more of the site. The storm flooded some of the **excavated** houses and washed away part of the village. Shortly after this, a sea wall was built to try to prevent further damage (see page 28).

Professor Childe

In 1927, a well-known **archaeologist** named Professor V. Gordon Childe became the first person to take organized **excavation** methods to the site. He and his team began by clearing the sand from the all of the buildings.

This is Skaill House, the home of William Watt. The ruins of Skara Brae were found on Watt's land.

Professor Childe can be seen here (circled). He is climbing out of an excavation on the site. This photograph was taken in 1930.

Disagreements

Some of the other experts looking at the excavation tried to get Professor Childe to write that the site was **Pictish**. The Picts were a tribe of people who lived in the late Iron Age, not Stone Age. But when Childe published a book called *A Pictish Village in Orkney*, his ideas were challenged by different archaeologists. They thought Skara Brae was much older than Pictish. Modern scientific methods have now been used to show that the site is older than Pictish, at nearly 5,000 years old.

Professor Childe wanted to dig down further into the site but was told not to. Once the sand was cleared from the houses, the Office of Works (part of the Government that looked after historic sites) stopped the excavation.

Skara Brae today

While Skara Brae was buried under the sand it was quite well protected. Uncovering the village **exposed** it to the weather. A sea wall was built to protect the village, but it is still at constant risk of damage. The site is now run by an organization called Historic Scotland. Historic Scotland is working to protect it.

The sea wall, shown here, was built using local stone and concrete.

Responsible tourism

Skara Brae is the best example of a **Neolithic** village in Northern Europe. Tourism is very important to the site – up to 80,000 people visit every year.

So many visitors to the site can wear away the paths and cause damage. Today there are raised pathways there. This allows visitors to look down into the **excavated** houses without causing damage. There is also a reconstruction (model) of one of the houses. This gives visitors a better idea of what life in a Neolithic village was like.

Timeline

BC

4200	First farming people arrive in Britain from Europe
About 4000	**Neolithic,** or New Stone Age, begins
3300–3200	Building begins at the Ness of Brodgar
3200	First building work begins at Skara Brae
3000–2900	Stones of Stenness are put in place
About 2800	First stones of Stonehenge are put in place
2700	Pyramids are built in Egypt
2600–2500	Ring of Brodgar is put in place
2500	Skara Brae is **abandoned**
About 2000	Neolithic period ends

AD

1850	Skara Brae is discovered
1930	First full **excavation** of Skara Brae is carried out by Professor V. Gordon Childe
1972–1973	Site is **excavated** by Dr David Clarke; Skara Brae is confirmed as Neolithic
2002	Large Neolithic site is found at Ness of Brodgar
2004–present	Excavations continue at Ness of Brodgar

Glossary

abandon leave someone or something behind with no plans to return

AD dates after the birth of Christ; these count upwards, so AD 20 is earlier than AD 25

alcove separate area of a room that is partly enclosed but set back into a wall

archaeologist scientist who studies human history by digging up people's buildings, belongings and even their bones

BC dates before the birth of Christ; these count downwards, so 3000 BC is earlier than 2500 BC

cure way of making food last longer by salting, smoking or drying

defensive something built or done in order to protect against attack

driftwood wood that has been washed up from the sea onto the shore

evidence object that proves something existed or happened

excavate uncover something by digging or removing soil

excavation act of excavating, or uncovering, something

expose when something is left bare so could be easily damaged

fertile land that produces healthy crops and plants

hearth floor of a fireplace

limpet type of sea snail that lives in water and has a cone-shaped shell

loch Scottish lake or part of the sea that is largely surrounded by land

midden prehistoric rubbish heap, or mound, mostly made up of bone, shell, stone and waste

mound small hill, usually made from piles of gravel, sand or rocks, and covered with earth and grass

Neolithic period in time that was the later part of the Stone Age

ochre type of metal (iron oxide) found in the earth, which is mixed with clay or sand to create different pigments

Orcadian relating to the Orkney islands or the people who live there

Pictish relating to the Picts, the people who lived in what is now northern and eastern Scotland during the late Iron Age

pigment powdered substance that can be mixed with oil or water to make a colouring material like paint or ink

prehistoric coming from a time before written history

settlement place where people make their homes

Find out more

Books

Changes in Britain from the Stone Age to the Iron Age (Early British History), Claire Throp (Raintree, 2015)

Life in the Stone Age, Bronze Age and Iron Age (A Child's History of Britain), Anita Ganeri (Raintree, 2014)

Websites

www.bbc.co.uk/scotland/learning/primary/skarabrae
This interactive website from the BBC has activities and videos about Skara Brae.

www.educationscotland.gov.uk/scotlandshistory/ earlypeople/skarabrae
This website about Scottish history includes photographs, illustrations and information about Skara Brae.

www.historic-scotland.gov.uk
Historic Scotland is responsible for taking care of Skara Brae and many other ancient sites across Scotland.

www.orkneyjar.com
This website includes contributions from the archaeologists who have been excavating the ancient sites in Orkney.

Index